Once Upon a Time in a Universe

For Luca

**IN LOVING MEMORY OF MY DAD...
MY FAITH HERO**

by Leanne Borrelli

Once upon a time in a universe, God wanted to create something beautiful. So He said:

"LET THERE BE LIGHT!"

And with a big BANG!
Light
Energy
and Love
filled the empty universe.

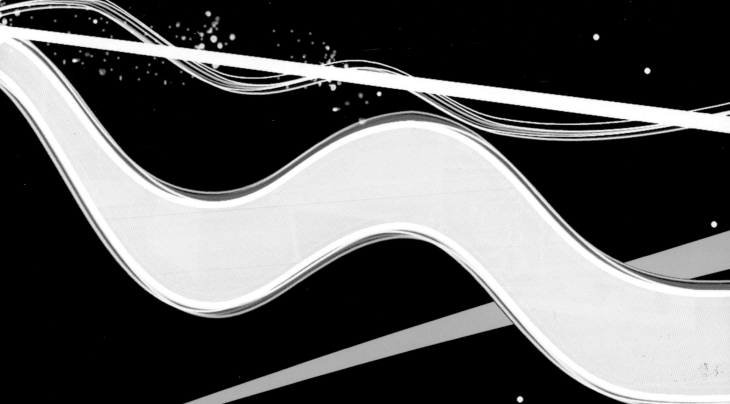

Later He created **LAND, WATER** and **PLANTS** of all kinds that gave this new world so much color and beauty... (What COLORS do you see here?)

...then came the **SUN**, **MOON** and **STARS**... and so many creatures to fill the oceans and birds to fly in the sky! (Can you find the face of Jesus? Where is it?)

The next day God let His imagination run **WILD** creating every animal you can think of: lions, puppies, elephants, kittens, lizards, zebras, monkeys, butterflies and more... (Now try to find each one!)

And finally, to complete His new world, He made ADAM and EVE - people like you and me! He loved Adam and Eve so much that He let them live in His favorite special GARDEN.

God asked Adam and Eve **not** to eat fruit from a certain special *tree*. But one day the people decided to eat fruit from exactly that tree. God, who sees EVERYTHING, had to punish them. So He sent them away from the garden never to return.

God knew the people would make mistakes. This *didn't stop* His love for them. So He decided to come up with another way to connect with the people. And He had **an idea!**

First, He called ABRAHAM. God asked Abraham to *trust* Him for lots of children to become His "CHOSEN PEOPLE" that He called **Israel.** *(Can you find the seven biggest stars?)*

Next, He brought Moses to a mountaintop and gave him ten rules on **two big stones.**

Israel DISOBEYED these rules a lot, but God **loved** them anyway and offered a system of forgiveness. Every time someone disobeyed, they had to go to the temple and send a lamb to heaven to be with God; then He would *forgive* their sin.

The people sinned so much that this system became very DIFFICULT
for God and for the people...but especially for the *lambs*.

To solve this problem, God sent some PROPHETS who told the people to stop disobeying God because He loved them and their sin made Him sad.

But instead of listening to the prophets, the people continued to have PARTIES and do what made them **happy**...
... because sometimes it's more fun to do what makes you happy then to do what is RIGHT...Right?

This story went on and on until finally **God** decided to do something almost unbelievable.

He decided to go to earth Himself as a PERSON – to breathe and walk and eat like the people, so that He could tell them in their own language how much He **loved** them.

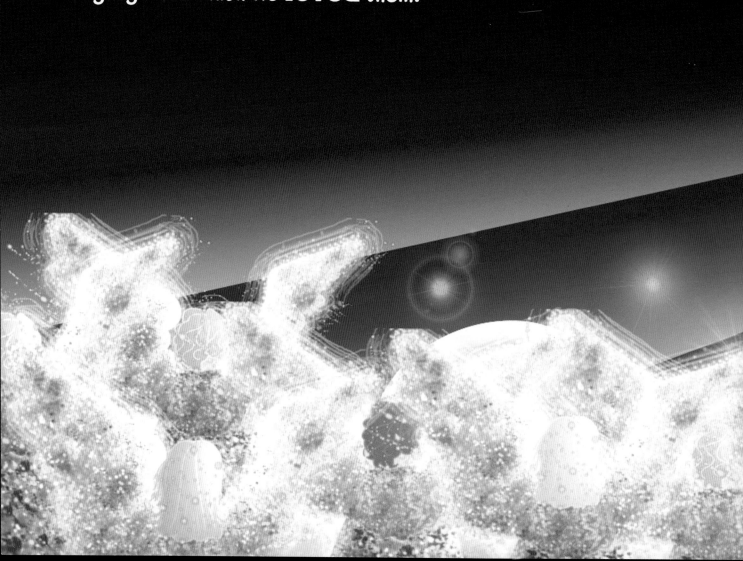

To do this, God had to become a baby. He chose a young woman named Mary to be His mom and a kind man named Joseph to be His earthly dad. He was born in a barn in a small village in Israel called BETHLEHEM.

They named the baby JESUS. He filled that night with so much joy that the stars and angels **sparkled** with hope!

Day after day that baby grew and became **BIG**, STRONG and REALLY SMART because He studied the word of God all the time.

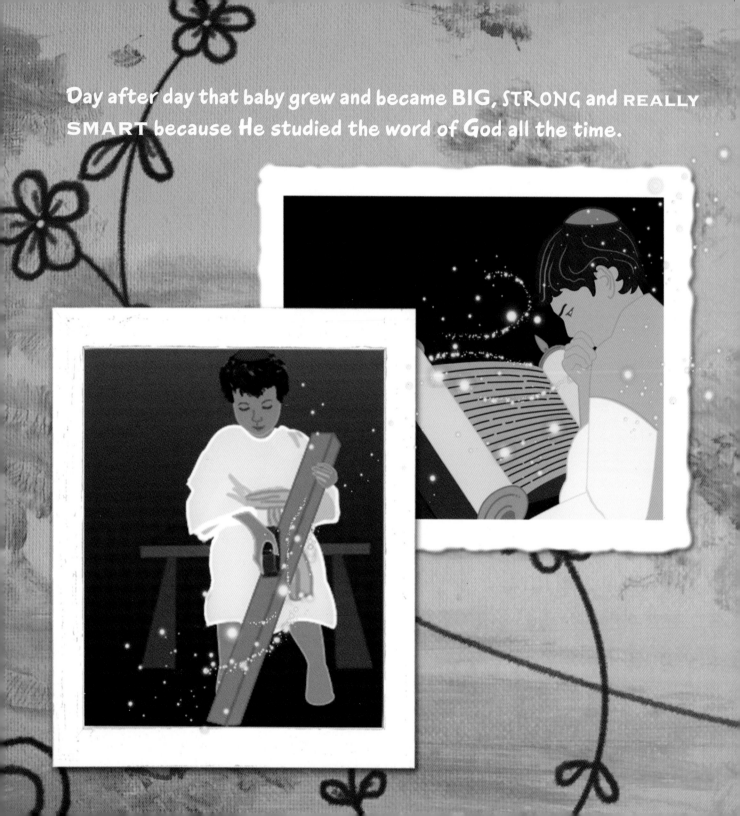

Jesus felt God's hand on His heart. And the more He studied God's word, the more He became full of joy. He understood that He wasn't just a prophet, but the *Son of God* who needed to share this message of **peace**, **love** and **hope** with the world!

Full of courage, He left home and started His ADVENTURE. He walked and walked... and everywhere He went He talked about God in a way the people had never heard before.

He healed lots of people. He brought a little girl who had died **back to life**; He calmed a storm by speaking to it; and He even WALKED ON WATER!

The people followed Jesus everywhere. He spoke about all their rules and said that only **ONE RULE** really matters:

Love God with all your heart and love your neighbor as yourself.

However, the religious leaders were not happy about the people following Jesus and forgetting about all their **rules**.

But Jesus continued to do miracles. He helped a little boy who couldn't walk... to **RUN!** He helped blind people SEE. And He brought His friend Lazarus back from the DEAD!

The religious leaders were worried about Jesus getting too **popular**. They wanted to get rid of Him, but they had to wait for the RIGHT MOMENT.

Jesus knew that He must suffer greatly to help people understand God's love. So He invited His closest friends to His last supper and told them He must suffer and die, but after THREE DAYS, He would **rise** again.

After dinner, He took His disciples to a GARDEN to pray. But one of His disciples told the religious leaders where Jesus was, away from all the people... Their MOMENT had come.

The guards **arrested** Him in the garden. Then the religious leaders found people who were AFRAID of them and ordered the people to **punish** Jesus.

He had to carry a heavy **cross** up a hill and no one could help Him. The Roman guards treated Him like a criminal and then...

... they hung Jesus on that cross. But even from the cross, He loved the people. He **prayed** to His Heavenly Father to FORGIVE them because they didn't understand who He was and what they were doing.

Then He closed His eyes and said, **"It is finished."** He was sure that His suffering was the ultimate display of God's great love for our world. Jesus died like a PERFECT sacrificial *Lamb*, gentle and innocent.

Then, just as He said, **three days** later, Jesus came **BACK** ... from the DEAD! The stone was rolled away and His tomb was *empty*! He greeted His friend Mary and proved that **God** can help man overcome ANYTHING!

A few days later, Jesus ate breakfast with His friends on the beach. And then HUNDREDS of people saw Jesus alive!

But He couldn't stay for long because His mission was complete - He showed man how to LOVE LIKE GOD. And now it was time to go home.

Home was with His Father in heaven; but He promised to come back. Then Jesus disappeared into the clouds and His friends told **everyone** they knew about Him - His miracles, His death and resurrection and how *wonderful* He was.

Since then, His story has been told for thousands of years, and now **you** know His story too.

So, with our eyes to the sky, let's thank God for **all** He has done. And if you ever need **anything,** just look up and ask. Like a good Father, God is always near, ready to help.

For God so loved the world that He gave His one and only Son, that whoever believes in Him shall not perish but have eternal life. John 3:16

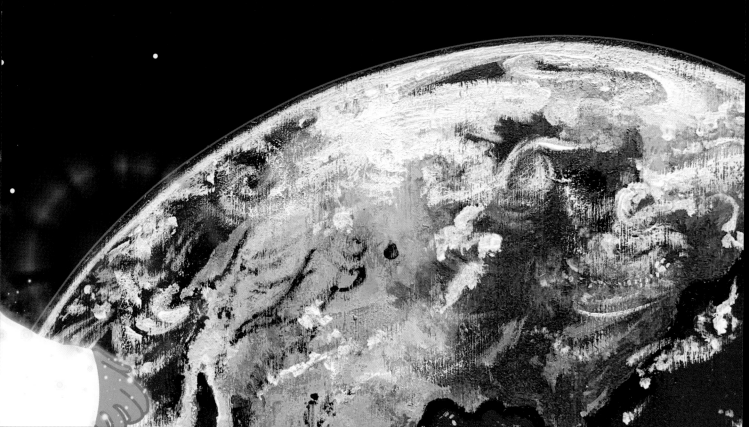

If you want to hold God's hand, be like Jesus and start an amazing faith adventure, try praying this...

Dear God, thank You for creating **EVERYTHING** - the sun, moon, trees, water, butterflies, kittens and so much more... And thank You for creating and loving me. Help me to always love others and do something great for You. I am ready for an **adventure**. In Jesus name, Amen.

For we are God's masterpiece. He has created us anew in Christ Jesus, so we can do the good things He planned for us long ago.
Ephesians 2:10

Let's Review...

1. Who created light, water, plants and animals?

2. What was the name of the first man and woman?

3. What did God give to Moses on the mountaintop?

4. What animal had to be sacrificed when someone broke God's rules?

   A. a lion   B. a lamb   C. a lizard

5. What was the name of God's son?

6. When Jesus was punished, what did he have to carry up a hill?

7. When Jesus died, what kind of animal was He compared to that was gentle and innocent?

   A. a dinosaur   B. a peacock   C. a lamb

8. After Jesus died, how many days later did He come back to life?

9. After Jesus left our earth, where did He go?

   A. Disneyland   B. Jurassic World   C. Heaven

10. While Jesus lived here on Earth, which of God's rules did He say was the most important?   How can **YOU** live this rule too?

ABOUT THE AUTHOR

Leanne Borrelli is a self-taught artist who always wanted to see the world and explore God's creation. She was raised in church in New Castle, Pennsylvania. She lost her way in college and beyond but God never let her go. Now, Leanne is an American living in Italy, a wife of a world-traveling gelato expert and a mother of a 4-year-old little boy named Luca. With a deep desire to teach Luca her most important life lessons in a simple book about Jesus, she wrote and illustrated "Once Upon a Time in a Universe."

Outside of creating and promoting the book, Leanne teaches English classes at a local preschool in Italy. She enjoys painting, interior decorating, organizing playdates with her son and his friends, walking the foothills of the Italian Alps appreciating the beauty of God's creation and dreaming up new ideas and adventures to try.

Her current motto is "Live Inspired."

For a reading by the author, feel free to check out Leanne's YouTube channel and follow along with your book. Search "Leanne Borrelli" on YouTube and choose the video of your preferred language. Enjoy!

WestBow Press books may be ordered through booksellers or by contacting:

WestBow Press
A Division of Thomas Nelson & Zondervan
1663 Liberty Drive
Bloomington, IN 47403
www.westbowpress.com
1 (866) 928-1240

Interior Graphics/Art Credit: Leanne Borrelli

ISBN: 978-1-9736-7676-8 (sc)
ISBN: 978-1-9736-7677-5 (e)

Library of Congress Control Number: 2019915609

Printed in the United States of America.

WestBow Press rev. date: 08/13/2020

WESTBOW
PRESS®
A DIVISION OF THOMAS NELSON
& ZONDERVAN